Fire on
the Water

Wendy A. Lewis

James Lorimer & Company Ltd., Publishers
Toronto

Copyright © 2007 by Wendy A. Lewis

All rights reserved. No part of this book may be reproduced or transmitted in any form or by any means, electronic or mechanical, including photocopying, or by any information storage or retrieval system, without permission in writing from the publisher.

James Lorimer & Company Ltd. acknowledges the support of the Ontario Arts Council. We acknowledge the support of the Government of Canada through the Book Publishing Industry Development Program (BPIDP) for our publishing activities. We acknowledge the support of the Canada Council for the Arts for our publishing program. We acknowledge the assistance of the OMDC Book Fund, an initiative of Ontario Media Development Corporation.

Cover design: Meghan Collins and Kate Moore

Library and Archives Canada Cataloguing in Publication

Lewis, Wendy A., 1966–
    Fire on the water : the red-hot career of superstar rower Ned Hanlan / Wendy Lewis.
(Recordbooks)

ISBN-13: 978-1-55028-973-2 (bound)
ISBN-13: 978-1-55028-972-5 (pbk.)

       1. Hanlan, Edward, 1855–1908 — Juvenile literature. 2. Rowers — Canada — Biography — Juvenile literature. I. Title. II. Series.

GV790.92.H35L49 2007   j797.12'3092   C2007-900359-1

James Lorimer & Company Ltd., Publishers
317 Adelaide Street West, Suite #1002
Toronto, ON
M5V 1P9
www.lorimer.ca

Distributed in the United States by:
Orca Book Publishers
P.O. Box 468
Custer, WA USA
98240-0468

Printed and bound in Canada

Fire on
the Water

J 797.123092 Hanla -L

Lewis, W.
Fire on the water.

PRICE: $9.95 (3559/ex   )

Contents

For my athletic niece and nephews,
Katie, Michael, and Brian Boehm

1 The Rowing Boy

The boy rowed until his scrawny arms ached, but his little boat did not budge. It was stuck on the beach of Toronto Island. He had helped his dad build it. They used a wooden plank and parts of old racing shells. But in the boy's mind, the toy was the real thing. The sand beneath his boat was the cool water of Toronto Bay. And he was a racing champion.

The boy was little Edward Hanlan, better known as Ned. He was born in 1855. When Ned was growing up, people loved to watch sculling and other kinds of rowing races. Huge crowds filled lakeshores, riverbanks, and steamers to cheer on scullers. The world's best were rich, famous, and adored by fans. They were the superstars of their time. Like Ned, many boys dreamed of becoming sculling champions when they grew up.

On that September day in 1860, Ned looked across the bay to the busy city wharves. The waterfront swarmed with people getting ready for a visit from the Prince of Wales. A big regatta was planned, with sailing and rowing races. Ned itched to get closer to the fun.

Ned knew he could row all the way to the city, as the bigger boys did. He had been rowing around the Island lagoons since he could walk and hold an oar. Though he was small for his age, he was strong. Soon he would be going to school on the mainland, and would have to get there by boat. Why wait?

Ned stepped off his toy boat. He pushed his family's skiff into the lake and rowed onto the bay. It was crowded with other rowboats, sailboats, schooners and steamers. Ned dodged them all, and arrived safely at the city's Market Wharf.

When he was older, Ned's fans would repeat the story of his first solo crossing from the Island to Toronto. Some may wonder if it really happened. Most agree that it did. Over time, young Ned's journey across the bay became a legend.

SCULLING AND SWEEPING

There are two types of rowing. In sculling, the athlete holds two oars, one in each hand. In sweep rowing, the athlete holds one oar in both hands.

People said he was born with oars in his hands. They said his baby carriage was a boat. They said the Island was the perfect place for a sculler to grow up. And they were right.

2 Boy of the Island

Ned's father, John Hanlan, came to Canada from Ireland. He worked as a fisherman on Lake Ontario. When John moved to Toronto Island, it was not yet a real island. It was joined to the mainland by a stretch of sand. A factory at The Narrows made soap, candles, and starch. Near the factory was a hotel. It became a popular spot for people from the city.

John preferred the central and western parts of the Island. They still had a wild beauty. The only people who lived in those areas were the lighthouse keeper, some fishermen, and their families. John and his wife, Ann, made their home there. They had four children: Mary Ann, Emily, Edward (Ned), and John.

At first, the Hanlans lived in a small shack. They were at the mercy of strong winds blowing off the lake. When Ned was a baby, their shack blew down in a storm. But the Hanlans did not give up. They piled their belongings on a raft and found a better place to rebuild. The spot became known as Hanlan's Point.

An even bigger storm tore up the Island two years later. The hotel at The Narrows was ripped apart. The hotelkeeper's family barely escaped. Massive waves scooped out the sand that joined the Island to the mainland. It was now a real island.

Storms did not make Ned afraid of the water. He was born loving it. A baby photo shows him sitting in a bowl, holding tiny toy oars. He learned to swim, row, and fish at an early age. Ned and his friends roamed the Island, barefoot and tanned. They caught fish in the lagoons and cooked them over driftwood fires.

The Island waters were part of Ned's playground, but they could also be dangerous. When Ned was seven, tragedy struck a fisherman's family. Teenager William Ward took his five young sisters sailing, and the boat flipped over. William survived. His sisters did not. After the accident, William became a lifesaver. If a boat was in trouble near the Island, he raced out in his rowboat to rescue the people on board. During his lifetime, William saved the lives of 164 people.

Ned was often reminded of other boating tragedies. The wrecks of the *Monarch* and the *Sophia* sat rotting offshore. When he was twelve, the *Jane Ann Marsh* sank during a fierce snowstorm. William and another fisherman, Bob Berry, tried to reach the sinking ship. Their own boat overturned three times in the rough, freezing water. Men on shore dragged them back to safety with a lifeline. Finally, William and Bob reached the ship. They had to break a layer of ice off the nearly frozen crew.

These dangers might keep some boys off the water, but not Ned. When he started school, he rowed himself to the mainland. He fished with his father. He took their catch to the city's market. Ned's early boat races were against other fishermen trying to get to the market first. He became very fast.

The Hanlans did well over the years. Ned's father became the Island's police constable. He also built a small, one-storey

ISLAND FERRY

The first ferry carrying people between Toronto and the Island was called a "horse ferry." Horses walked on a treadmill to power the boat!

hotel. His main love, though, was fishing. Before long, he went back on the water and left his family to run the hotel. Hanlan's Hotel became a gathering place for Islanders. Mainlanders liked it too.

Island families had fun when the harbour froze in the winter. They slid, skated, and fished through holes in the ice. The most thrilling winter sport was iceboating. Skates were attached to the bottoms of sailboats. Boaters could zip along the ice at eighty kilometres (fifty miles) an hour! The Toronto

An engraving by Rowley W. Murphy of William Ward and Robert Berry rescuing the crew of a boat.

Rowing Club even held iceboat regattas.

In summer, the Island was taken over by mainlanders. They packed the beaches for picnics, sunbathing, and boating. The biggest crowds came to watch the boat races at the Toronto Regatta. Races took place off the Island's shores. Decorated yachts and steamers filled the bay. Bands played, steam whistles blew, and everyone had a grand time.

Fishermen's races were for crews of three men. William Ward and Bob Berry often took part. There were also races for double scullers, in-rigged boats, out-rigged boats, and sailboats. There were silly races in tubs and a game called Duck Hunt. One rower was the "duck" while the others chased him.

One race was taken very seriously. It was the single-scull race for the Championship of Toronto Bay. The winner was considered the best sculler around. Young Ned dreamed of rowing across the bay to victory.

3 Champion of Toronto Bay

When Ned was a boy, one man was almost always the champion of Toronto Bay. Thomas Tinning was from mainland Toronto. Like William Ward, Tinning used his rowing skills to save lives. He led a volunteer crew. They used a six-metre (twenty-foot) lifeboat from New York.

William and Tinning once argued about how to carry out a rescue. William wanted to row to a sinking ship during a bad storm. Tinning said the water was too rough for rescue boats to head out. They settled it with a fistfight on the beach. (In the end, they shook hands and did the rescue together after the storm eased up.) However, the rivalry ended there. William never challenged Tinning for his championship title. Neither did Ned — he was still too young. But one Islander did: the fisherman Bob Berry.

It was 1868, and Ned was thirteen. He was still small for his age, but his lively nature made him seem bigger. He cheered with the other Islanders when Bob Berry joined the starting line of the big race.

Bob was clearly an outsider. His boat was rough looking next to the sleek racing shells. He was the only African Canadian in the race. He was also poor. But Bob was a large, strong man. He was used to rowing through choppy waves, like those in the bay on race day. *The Globe* reported: "The coloured man, Berry, whose boat is much larger and heavier than any of the others, said he would row in any weather."

Tinning agreed, but some rowers pulled out of the race. Among them was a big-time sculler named Tom Louden. Though Tinning was the local champion, most people had bet on Louden to win. Finally, the water calmed a bit and the remaining rowers took off.

Bob had great strength on his side. He also wanted to prove himself. In spite of his heavy boat, he quickly pulled ahead. To the

RACING SHELLS

In the 1800s, boat builders created special rowboats, called shells, for racing. Shells are long, narrow, and lightweight. The narrower the boat, the faster it moves through water. A shell's oars mount on outriggers. Outriggers attach to the sides of the boat.

shock of many, Bob crossed the finish ahead of Tinning.

The Islanders went wild. One of their own was Champion of Toronto Bay! But Bob did not keep his title for long. Tinning claimed that Bob did not round the buoy correctly at the turn. The race judges agreed. The mainlander was made champion once again.

Ned was a friendly lad but he also had a temper. No doubt his voice rose above the other protests when Bob lost his title. Such disputes were all too common in the rowing world.

Dirty tricks were also common. Gamblers bet a lot of money on sculling races. Scullers took bribes to "throw" a race. Boats were destroyed and death threats were made. Some athletes were even poisoned. It was a dangerous business.

When Ned was a teenager, he would have read newspapers to keep up with the rowing scene. The Great Race of 1869 was big news. It was a sculling showdown on the River Thames in England. Top teams from American and English universities competed. At stake was a lot of money and national pride. The Americans had food smuggled into their hotel so they wouldn't be poisoned. To the relief of the English, Oxford won.

A New Brunswick team also made front-page news. The four-man crew took on Europe's best sculling teams. The race was held at the World Exposition in Paris. The Europeans had the latest boats and spiffy uniforms. The Canadians wore plain clothing and rowed a heavy boat. But they won easily, talking and laughing as they crossed the finish line.

A sculler from Nova Scotia made headlines too. Like Bob Berry, George Brown was a fisherman. He had won Halifax's championship race so often that he was given the title belt to keep forever. Brown raced in the world championship of single-sculls. His opponent was Joseph Sadler of England. Sadler won but was accused of cheating. He refused to race in a rematch. If he had, Brown might have been the first Canadian world champion — in any sport. Sadly, Brown died before he had the chance to challenge for the title again.

As Canadian scullers gained world fame, rowing became even more popular. Ned was not yet old enough to enter the big races. But he raced against the other Island boys. He helped his older friends, like Bob Berry, train. He practiced. He learned. He dreamed.

When Ned was fifteen, he watched Bob win the Championship of Toronto Bay. This time, no one took the title from Bob. Ned even beat Tom Louden, the gamblers' favourite. Now the newspapers talked about Bob's talent instead of the colour of his skin.

There were many differences between Bob and Ned. Bob was tall and brawny. Ned was small and wiry. Ned would never be as strong as Bob. And yet, they had some things in common. Both were underdogs. Both came from poor backgrounds. Much like African Canadians, the Irish faced prejudice in Canada. Ned was surely proud of his friend. Perhaps he thought: If he can do it, I can too.

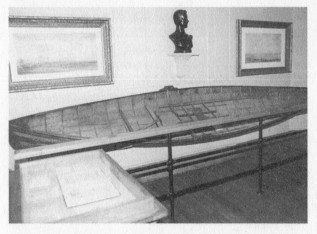

This early racing shell of Ned's is very different from the "needle boats" he used later.

4 Champion of Ontario

The date of Ned's first official race is a mystery. Many reports claim he raced with a fishermen's crew in 1871. He was sixteen then. But Ned's name was not among the rowers listed in the newspaper. The next year, a "J. Hanlon" was listed. Ned's last name was often misspelled early in his rowing career. But who was *J*? It was not Ned's father. He had died a few months earlier. It could not be Ned's brother, John, either. He was too young. Was J. Hanlon really Ned?

There is more to the mystery. William Ward had always raced in the Toronto Regatta. In 1872, he did not. Bob Berry played only a small role. He entered the fishermen's race but skipped the sculling matches. Something had changed in the Toronto rowing scene. The Toronto Regatta was put on hold. Rowing news in Toronto all but vanished for four years.

An 1876 issue of *The Globe* offers the reason. It reports a deep rift between professional and amateur rowers. Professionals race for money; amateurs do not. The amateurs were upset that so many pros had joined the rowing club. The pros also carried off most of the prizes. The amateurs felt their sport had been ruined by money. So, they created a new club of their own in Toronto: the Argonaut Rowing Club.

After his father died, Ned had to support his family. He fished and helped run the hotel. In his spare time, he kept up his training. He won skiff races against his friends and other fishermen. He tried out different boats and rowing methods.

At eighteen, Ned built his own racing shell. By then, the Championship of Toronto Bay was on again. Years earlier, people had been shocked when Bob Berry joined the scullers at the starting line. What did they think when the small Irish fisherman's son rowed up in a homemade shell?

Two very talented scullers were racing, William McKen and Sam Williams. Bets were placed on them to win. Ned was ignored — until he started to row. Years of practice and racing for fun paid off. The blades of his oars sliced the waves. His shell skimmed through the water. Stroke by stroke, he pulled ahead of the talented two. When he came to a rest, Ned Hanlan was the new Champion of Toronto Bay.

Ned's next challenge was to race the famous Tom Louden. Although Thomas Tinning had beat him, Louden was still a top sculler. The race took place on Hamilton Bay. Ned's powerful strokes drove him past Louden to the finish.

No one had expected the newcomer to do well. Louden was the most surprised of all. Who was this puny, young upstart? He challenged Ned to a rematch on Toronto Bay. Beating Ned in front of a hometown crowd would put him in his place.

The racecourse was only one-and-a-half kilometres (one mile) long. Louden was a master at short sprints. He — and the gamblers — thought there would be no contest.

Louden offered Ned a side bet of $100. It was common for rowers to place side bets with each other. It showed that they were serious about the race. One hundred dollars was a lot of money for Ned. (It would be about $2,000 today.) If he lost the race, he would have trouble coming up with the money. Still, he accepted the bet and rowed to win.

Louden was stunned when Ned again finished first. The young man seemed very lucky. Lucky — and $100 richer.

Ned's friends and family knew that it was not luck. It was skill and hard work. They had been watching Ned since he was a toddler. If he wanted something, he made it happen. At eighteen, he was an able fisherman and hotel operator. Now he wanted to become a professional sculler. Everyone believed he would do his best.

Would his best be enough, though? Most champion scullers had money, coaches, and trainers. They had time to practice, the best boats and gear. How could a kid from the Island compete with that?

Louden challenged Ned a third time.

The other wins might have been flukes. Anything can happen on race day — to a sculler, his boat, the water, or the weather. One rower could gain a slight edge. Louden was sure he would win the next race.

This time, the Lord Dufferin Medal was the prize up for grabs. Also at stake was the championship of Ontario. The race would take place on Ned's home waters, Toronto Bay. Another top sculler, James Douglas, would be rowing too. Torontonians were

CHOOSING THE COURSE

In Ned's time, rowers decided the lengths of their racecourses. They ranged from one-and-a-half to eight kilometres (one to five miles), or more. Sometimes they were straight-aways. Sometimes they included a turn. Rowers signed contracts agreeing to the terms of the races, including length, weather conditions, and prize money.

thrilled — and torn. Louden and Douglas were both first-rate rowers. Could Ned really win again?

The three-kilometre (two-mile) race was set for August 15, 1874. Ned had turned nineteen the month before. His boyish face and small size made him look younger. He was just under five foot nine. He weighed about 150 pounds. Most great scullers, like Louden and Douglas, were much bigger. Many were more than six feet tall and two hundred pounds. But Ned's skill shone through. His stroke was long and smooth. He not only kept pace with the bigger men, he beat them all.

Ned won Ontario's top prize for single-scull racing. It was a great day for the young sculler, for Torontonians, and for Islanders. It was not a great day for those who had bet on Louden and Douglas to win. Soon after his third defeat to Ned, Louden gave up single-scull racing.

5 The Hanlan Club

A group of important businessmen took an interest in Ned's rowing career. One of them was Colonel Albert D. Shaw, the American consul. He looked after America's interests in Toronto. Another was David Ward, William Ward's older brother. David was a pawnbroker, someone who lends money. He was later called the "discoverer of Ned Hanlan." These men had spotted Ned's talent. They believed that with the right support, he could win even bigger races.

The group formed the Hanlan Club. They took care of the business side of Ned's rowing career. They booked his races and dealt with the contracts. They bought him the best gear. Now Ned could focus on training and racing. As *The Mail* put it, all Ned had to do was "row, eat, exercise and sleep."

The Hanlan Club's support gave Ned new respect in rowing circles. It showed that he was not just a poor fisherman out to make prize money. He was a serious athlete, and one to watch.

One of the first boats the Club bought for Ned was Tom Louden's racing shell. They fitted it with a new invention: the sliding seat.

Before Ned's time, rowing shells had seats that did not move. A rower's upper body did all the work. That is why most top scullers were tall, broad men. In the

1850s, they started using a different part of their bodies — their legs. Pushing with their legs gave each pull of the oars extra power. The more push, the more power. The more power, the faster the shell moved through the water. With each leg thrust, the scullers slid back and forth. They started to grease the seats of their shells. They also had to wear special padding on their backsides!

Two men invented the sliding seat, Walter Brown and J.C. Babcock. They did not work together; they just happened to invent the same thing at the same time. By

STAYING IN SHAPE

The Hanlan Club gave Ned all the latest equipment, such as the newest version of the indoor rowing machine. It helped Ned keep his rowing muscles in shape during the winter when Toronto Bay was frozen over.

1871, Babcock's seat was listed in the *Illustrated Catalogue and Oarsman's Manual*. The seat moved on two greased tracks. It gave a sculler more thrust and speed. This helped a small athlete like Ned compete with larger men. But it was tricky to use. Most rowers liked the old way better — until Ned showed them how to do it right.

Backed by the Hanlan Club, Ned took part in races all over Ontario. When he turned twenty-one, the Club felt he was ready for a new challenge: the Centennial Regatta in Philadelphia. Top American and Canadian scullers would be competing there. Ned was entered to race with the pros. The prize money was $800 — a fortune to someone like Ned. He made up his mind to win.

Only one thing could slow him down: the police. There was a warrant out for his arrest.

6 From Outlaw to Hero

Booze caused many problems in the 1800s. Some people called it "demon drink" and tried to have it outlawed. Laws kept changing about when and where liquor could be sold. Hanlan's Hotel had a license to serve liquor, but many Islanders wanted to have whiskey at home too.

Ned started bootlegging liquor, selling it to people outside his hotel's licensed area. This made him popular with customers, but unpopular with police.

He was not the only one. William Ward ran a hotel now too, and was caught bootlegging. Lucky for William, he was well respected for his lifesaving efforts. The charges were dropped. Too bad Ned's champion status did not help him the same way.

Ned went into hiding. He couldn't train properly because the police were watching for him. The date of the Centennial Regatta drew closer. Ned feared the police would nab him when he left Toronto. Two days before he was to leave, they spotted him at the Toronto Rowing Club. The police rushed in the front door to grab Ned. He slipped out the back and hopped into a rowboat. On land, the police might have been able to catch him. But on the water? Not a chance.

Ned rowed with fury. A steamer was crossing the bay on its way to the United States. When Ned reached the ship, he climbed a rope ladder hanging down its side. The people on board couldn't believe

Ned as a baby and early in his racing career.

it. Neither could the police. It was a perfect getaway — and good practice for the race.

Ned's trainer brought his racing shell across the border. Then they set off for Philadelphia, where they met up with the Hanlan Club. Whatever the Club may have thought of Ned's stunt, they were proud of him too. He had the kind of spark needed to win big races. He'd need that spark to beat the best pros.

Ned won his first heat easily. Winners of the first heats went on to the second heats, then to the final race. Few Americans had heard of Ned before. Now people were buzzing about the young Canadian. They praised his graceful stroke. They were wowed by his mastery of the sliding seat.

Ned's second heat really got people talking. He was up against two American rowing stars, Pat Luther and Fred Plaisted. Ned started off pulling well. All of a sudden, he stopped. He calmly looked around to see how far there was to go. Scullers never did that during races. Of course, Ned had his own way of doing things. He picked up his oars and started rowing again. He seemed relaxed as he took long, easy strokes. A fuming Plaisted worked hard to keep up. But Ned won the heat.

Another great Canadian rower made it into the final race. He was Alex Brayley from New Brunswick. Ned's fans in Toronto waited by the telegraph office to hear the latest results. Brayley's fans did the same in the Maritimes. Canadians across the country held their breath. They hoped at least one of their men would beat the Americans.

Ned not only won, he set a new record. He finished the five-kilometre (three-mile) race in twenty-one minutes, nine and a half seconds.

Ned had left Toronto an outlaw. He

returned a hero. The SS *City of Toronto* brought him back in style. On the Island, two huge bonfires burned in his honour. A cheering crowd met him at the mainland dock. A band played "See the Conquering Hero Comes." The newspapers said that if he were a general who had led his troops to victory, he would not have had a bigger welcome home.

Ned's fans lifted him onto a racing shell. It had been decorated and mounted on a fire wagon. Friends stood around him with oars held high. The crowd got bigger as Ned was carried through the city. The parade grew so large, "the crush was something terrible," reported *The Globe*.

The Mayor presented him with a silver medal and a gold watch. For all his spark, Ned was shy about making speeches. His thanks were brief but sincere. People found his modesty charming. *The Globe* described him as "gracious, kindly, clean, humorous, honest and sporting."

Bootlegger Ned was now Toronto's favourite boy. Sporting fans loved him. The newspapers loved him. Young ladies especially loved him. But what about the police? They were out in great numbers that night — not to arrest Ned, but to control the large crowds. Ned had made his city and country proud. The warrant for his arrest was quietly filed in the trash.

7 Standing Up to the Big Boys

One young lady captured Ned's heart. Margaret "Maggie" Gordon Sutherland was from Nova Scotia. The eighteen-year-old was Ned's most loyal fan. They married and made Toronto Island their home base. Whenever she could, Maggie travelled with Ned to his races.

Ned continued to butt heads with the police over how he ran Hanlan's Hotel. In the summer of 1877, they shut it down for a while. Some people said that

Ned was treated unfairly. Others felt he was too headstrong and needed to be taught a lesson.

Ned spent most of the summer racing in New York State. After his success with the sliding seat, other scullers had put them on their boats. Ned was still the master, though. He usually wore a blue racing shirt, which earned him the nickname "The Boy in Blue." The Americans loved watching Ned race. It was fun to see a small man out-row bigger scullers. And Ned knew it. He grinned, winked, and waved as he crossed the finish line.

Before long, Ned got into hot water again.

Fred Plaisted was still stinging from how Ned had shown him up at the Centennial Regatta. Race planners played up the rivalry. They arranged a grudge match between Ned and Plaisted at the Silver Lake Regatta in Boston.

Ned lost, but it wasn't his fault. He had to stop rowing when one of his outriggers snapped. Had someone messed with it? Furious, Ned watched a smiling Plaisted row past him to the finish line.

Another race was set for two weeks later. All the competitors were invited back. Only Plaisted did not come. Ned won easily against the other two scullers. The Hanlan Club sent another challenge to Plaisted. Again, he did not accept it. Finally, Ned and Plaisted met at the July Fourth Regatta in Boston. It did not go well.

Twelve scullers crowded the racecourse. Before long, it was like bumper cars on water. Ned collided with Frenchy Johnson. Plaisted shot into the lead. As he rounded the buoy, Ned got in his way. Plaisted alerted the judges, who yelled at Ned. He yelled back in what a Boston newspaper called an "exceedingly unbecoming" way. (This likely meant that

Ned used a four-letter word.) Ned continued on his course and slammed into Plaisted's boat. Then he ran into Johnson again. The angry judges stopped the race and told the scullers to pull home — carefully. Plaisted finished first, Johnston second. Ned was seventh.

Ned claimed that he was fouled. Plaisted and Johnson insisted that Ned had fouled them. The judges ruled in favour of the Americans. Ned was banned from racing in Boston. He appealed the decision, and the ban was lifted. But the event left a black mark on his record.

Back home, Ned faced Wallace Ross in a race for the Championship of Canada.

NAMES FOR NED

In addition to "the Boy in Blue," newspapers called Edward Hanlan "the little giant" and "the Aquatic King."

Ross was a tall, muscular sculler from New Brunswick. Many people thought he was the best sculler in the country. Ned was sure he could beat him. The Hanlan Club thought so too.

The championship race was set to take place on Toronto Bay. Betting was high in Toronto and in the Maritimes. The prize purse was a whopping $1,000 (about $20,000 today).

Anything that might affect the outcome of the race was important news. During a practice, Ross's boat was damaged by an object in the water. Rumours spread in New Brunswick that Ned's people or gamblers were behind the incident. Maritime newspapers urged Ross to come home. Ross refused. The race would go on.

On October 13, 1877, tens of thousands of people filled boats and lined the waterfront. To their disappointment, the race was called off due to high winds and rough water. Two days later, they gathered again. The Toronto crowd applauded politely for Ross as he took his place in his boat. They cheered themselves hoarse when Ned appeared. He was their hometown hero. Even his racing shell was made locally by the Wharin brothers.

Ned and Ross had very different rowing styles. Ross rowed in the traditional way with short, choppy strokes. *The Globe* reported that he jerked himself along "with his elbows flying." In contrast, Ned burned ahead "like a small steam engine." He had time to stop and rest, speak to friends, and blow kisses to the crowd — and he still won by thirty boat lengths.

There were grumblings in New Brunswick, but no one questioned whether the race had been fair. Ned was the Champion of Canada.

Ned had his showdown with Fred Plaisted in May, 1878. The three-kilometre (two-mile) straightaway race would take place on Toronto Bay. Once again, the prize was $1,000. Newspapers billed the race as a match between Canada and America. Ned trained hard for it all winter. He looked forward to racing — and beating — Plaisted again. Plaisted was just as sure he would be the victor.

Before the race, everyone wanted to see the rival scullers. Ned and Plaisted greeted their fans at the Royal Opera House and Lyceum Theater in Toronto. Then they took the train to Hamilton. The crowd at the Adelaide Street rink met them with a standing ovation.

Many Hamilton fans came to Toronto by train to see the big race. Low train fares were offered for the special occasion. *The Globe* reported that "forty thousand spectators saw or tried to see the race." Front-row seats went to passengers on twenty steamers that were "crowded like a beehive." More than three hundred and fifty small boats "swarmed like mosquitoes" along the course. Some people even perched in the riggings of schooners. People covered the wharves, grain elevators, and roofs of waterfront buildings. One poor man fell off the City Elevator roof and was killed.

The race began at 6 o'clock. This time, there was no fouling or flares of temper. Maybe the two contenders had new respect for each other. Maybe they were just intent on winning.

The race was close. Plaisted was "putting in sharp, heavy work at the rate of 30 strokes to the minute," *The Globe* reported. Ned was "pulling a long full stroke at 28 to the minute." Plaisted's oar sliced the water with great power, but then his stroke petered out. Ned kept up his stroke, never pausing. In the end, Plaisted "had clearly pumped himself out," and

Ned won. As *The Globe* summed up: "No man can row in Plaisted's style and win against Hanlan."

Ned with racing shells at his boathouse on Toronto Island.

8 Taking on America

Not only had Ned Hanlan defeated Fred Plaisted, a Canadian had defeated an American. The time was right for Ned to represent Canada in an official race between the two countries. He challenged Ephraim "Eph" Morris, the Champion of America, for his title.

Today, championship titles are usually held for a year. In Ned's time, champions could be challenged at any time. And a Canadian could challenge the top American or Englishman to become champion of those countries.

The race between Ned and Morris was set for June 20, 1878. The course was on the Allegheny River in Pittsburgh, Pennsylvania. Newspapers hailed the race as "the great sporting event of the season."

A large group of wealthy Torontonians followed Ned and the Hanlan Club to Pittsburgh. They brought their eager support — and lots of money to bet on Ned. Newspapers reported that Canadians wagered between $60,000 and $300,000 in total. Ned's head must have been spinning.

So was the Allegheny River. The river had swift currents and swirling eddies, but Morris knew his way around them. Recent heavy rains made the river extra high, fast, and littered with driftwood. The worst of it was cleaned up by race time, but Ned still had to learn the ins and outs of the currents.

Fans read in the newspapers about Ned's typical training day. Walk five kilometres (three miles). Eat a hearty breakfast. Take a short rest. Head out on the river for a training session at a medium speed. Rubdown. Write letters, read the newspaper, or visit friends. Lunch at twelve sharp: lean meat, stale bread, and a glass or two of chilled Scotch ale. Rest for an hour. Walk eight kilometres (five miles). Another rubdown. Supper. Head out on the racecourse. Paddle the first half nice and easy, row the second half at race speed. In bed by nine o'clock. Sleep for ten hours.

On the day of the race, strangers

TRAIN SMARTER, NOT HARDER

Ned was focused and relaxed in training. One reporter suggested that Ned did not work as hard as other scullers did. Ned replied, "There is no man living works harder than I do in training, but I just put in the work where I know it is wanted."

swarmed the city. Booths and tents were set up to sell food, drinks, and souvenirs. Gambling stations and games like Wheel-of-Fortune did a great deal of business.

When Ned and Morris came out of their boathouses, the crowd cheered politely for Ned and wildly for Morris. This was no surprise. Of course the Americans would support their own athlete. And Ned liked Morris. He was a fair man and a hard worker.

Morris did not tower over Ned as most scullers did. They were about the same height, though Morris was heavier set with a broad upper body. Next to Morris, wiry Ned was referred to as "the little fellow." *The Globe* reported, "Morris pulls a very true and steady stroke with more arm and less body action than Hanlan. In fact Morris' style, though cleaner and sharper, is very much like that of Wallace Ross."

Ned's boat was a new, Spanish-cedar

shell. It was nine metres (about thirty feet) long and only thirty centimetres (twelve inches) wide. Morris raced in a boat made of many sheets of paper shaped over a mold. It was sealed with waterproof glue-resin.

The scullers took off from the starting line. Ned pulled thirty-six strokes a minute in his long, sweeping style. Morris pulled thirty-nine strokes a minute, using his powerful arms to propel him. Ned took the lead. Morris continued to pull hard and fast. *The Globe* reported that "Hanlan was leading by nearly seven lengths, and taking it easy, while Morris had his teeth set and was pulling as if for his life."

Ned paused a few times to let the American catch up. He waved to friends when he saw them on the riverbank. Near the end, Ned slowed to twenty-eight strokes a minute. He still won by three boat lengths. Afterwards, Morris came to Ned's boathouse to congratulate him. One of the ever-present reporters from *The Globe* recorded their chat.

"'It's all right, I suppose, Eph,' said Ned.

'I didn't see you do anything wrong,' Morris replied. He offered a smile and a handshake, admitting that he knew early in the race he couldn't win. 'But,' he told Ned, 'I thought I would … give you all the work I could.'

'That you did,' said Ned. 'It's the hardest race I have ever had.'"

He gave Morris a parting gift: a beautiful pair of oars made in Toronto.

Ned was now the American champion. Another big celebration was waiting for him at home. *The Mail* reported that all the Toronto ladies wanted to be introduced to him, while the men just stared at him in awe.

The partying did not last too long. Across the ocean, Ned's next big challenge was waiting for him: the Championship of England.

9 The Boy in Blue Races Britain's Best

The British loved rowing almost as much as they loved tea. It was part of their culture, history, and national identity. They had been racing rowboats since the 1700s. From common river-taxi drivers to students at Oxford and Cambridge universities, the British had a passion for sculling. They studied the sport, practised it, improved it, and shone at it. Rowing was theirs. Ned and the Hanlan Club knew it would be a great victory if a

Canadian beat Britain's top sculler.

Canada was still a young country. Officially, it was only twelve years old. Many British still viewed the new country as their "kid." Ned was nervy to challenge the English champion, William Elliott. But much of Ned's success came from being nervy. He tried things people did not think were possible. Americans loved Ned for his funny antics during races. But what would the proper British people think?

Almost no one in England knew about Ned. The Hanlan Club wanted to create excitement for the race against Elliott. So, first they matched Ned with another sculler. John Hawdon was one of Britain's best. Beating him would show off Ned's skill. The race was set for May 5, 1879, on the River Tyne.

Newspapers reported details about Ned's health, training routine, and boat problems. A new shell arrived from North

America, but it was too heavy and leaked. Luckily, Ned found a good boat builder close to where he trained. He ordered a new shell and it was ready just a few days later. Ned loved it. He called it the *Toronto*.

"Interest in the Hanlan-Hawdon match increases daily," reported *The Globe*, "and the practice of the oarsmen on the Tyne attracts large crowds."

Ned's old rival Fred Plaisted was also in England. He practiced with Ned. Locals admired Ned's "graceful style and swing of the rowing" but found Plaisted's style sloppy and "slovenly."

The weather was cold and cloudy for May. It even snowed! That didn't keep Ned off the water. He rowed with Plaisted each morning and afternoon, took a brisk walk, and then rowed again each evening. But Ned was careful not to overtrain, as he felt Hawdon was doing.

On race day, the British crowds were

amazed to see the little Canadian arrive at the finish line first, looking as fit and fresh as when he started. "Hawdon was trained to death," Ned said later. "When I stopped in the race and looked back at him, I … thought to myself, 'What a sack of bones!' It was a shame to train so, as Hawdon is a good man."

Ned was now big news in England. The date for the British championship race was set for June 16, 1879. William Elliott trained hard. He tried to master the new style of rowing that was making Ned famous in England.

Early in June, St. John's Catholic School gave a concert in Ned's honour. The students cheered loud and long when Ned walked onto the stage. The reverend presented him with a gold Maltese cross to show how much they admired his sculling. Ned thanked them warmly. He said that he meant to win the race, but that Mr.

Elliott was one of the finest rowers he had ever seen.

On race day, those students were among thousands who crowded the banks of the River Tyne. Some had camped overnight to get a good spot. Many arrived on special trains from London and other towns. Others came on foot. So many people were crossing the railroad tracks that the trains had to be stopped.

Rickety stands lined the banks for those who could pay for seats. Men and boys clung to the bridge supports. *The Globe* reported that the river "was alive with craft of every sort." Barges, rowboats, and steamers were packed with fans. It was an accident waiting to happen — and one did. Twenty daring boys tried to balance on an old raft and flipped into the water. They survived with a "hearty fright and a ducking" and a few "cuffs from the police and boatmen, who had hurried to their rescue."

The police cleared the racecourse. The challenger and the champion took their places at the start. Ned wore his usual blue racing shirt. Elliott wore no shirt. The crowd was in awe of the sight of his huge muscles. He was the picture of strength.

The Englishman was upset, though. So many people assumed Ned would win that there was little gambling on who would come first. Instead, they bet on how far behind Elliot would be when Ned crossed the finish line. Elliott called to his friends that he would take three-to-one odds that he'd lead the whole race. It must have hurt when no one took his offer.

Both scullers were eager to get underway. The referee called three false starts before the race finally began. Ned shot ahead, pulling forty-two strokes a minute. *The Globe* described Ned passing Elliot "as easily as a steam vessel does a sailing boat." Elliott pulled forty strokes a minute to catch up. Ned slowed to thirty-eight, but his stroke was so perfect that he still travelled faster than Elliott. "He sculled with grace and finish," *The Globe* said, "recovering like lightning, keeping his boat on an even keel, and seeming to almost lift her out of the water at every stroke." Elliott rowed with immense strength, but he splashed often and slipped back into his "old, short, vigorous style."

The Hanlan Club reported that Ned "kept well ahead in smooth water, and properly 'slowed down' where it was lumpy." He then stopped "when some ugly waters hopped into his shell." The water was soaked up by sponges, which he threw overboard to lighten the boat. "All this was done in the coolest manner."

Ned also slowed down to let Elliott catch up. Many British did not realize Ned sometimes slowed on purpose. They thought he had worn himself out. When

Ned stopped rowing completely, the crowd fell silent. Something was wrong. Scullers do not stop in the middle of a race! They watched Ned checking to see how far he had to go. He was still quite a distance from the finish line. Elliott could overtake him if he pumped hard, which he did. The gap between them closed. Then Ned smiled at the crowd, picked up his oars, and took off.

"Hanlan's final spurt," *The Globe* reported, "was ... the grandest piece of rowing ever seen on any English waters."

Elliott had raced like a champion, but it wasn't enough to beat the Boy in Blue.

Ned's boat crossed the finish line several lengths ahead of Elliott's. Ned could have finished the race much faster. But he still beat the previous record for the River Tyne racecourse by fifty-five seconds.

The London *Daily Telegraph* wrote, "A fisherman from Toronto, in Canada, has made mincemeat of one of the sturdiest and most athletic pitmen who ever went into training upon the Tyne."

The Newcastle *Chronicle* added, "Our best sculler has been beaten by a better man … Canada has reason to be 'proud of her boy'."

Ned was a gracious winner. He told the crowd it was an honour to be their champion. He said that Elliott was the best man he had ever rowed against. He thanked the English for their kind welcome. It was quite a speech. Clearly, Ned's public speaking had improved along with his rowing.

The Hanlan Club said Ned's "modest and gentlemanly bearing while in England won him a host of friends." Never before had a Canadian sculler received such praise and honour in England.

Some American newspapers seemed to forget where Ned was from. They bragged about "our American champion, Hanlan" without mentioning he was Canadian.

The *Ottawa Free Press* thought Ned should be knighted.

Of course, the most excited fans were the ones back home in Toronto.

Three hundred people joined Ned on the steamer *Chicora* for the final part of the journey home. As the *Chicora* crossed Lake Ontario, it was met by many small and large boats. By the time they rounded Toronto Island, the fleet was five kilometres (three miles) long. *The Globe* reported, "cheer after cheer went rolling

CARD COLLECTING

Champion scullers used to appear on trading cards. The cards were not included in packs of gum or candy. They came in packs of cigarettes! The Ned Hanlan card was a hot collector's item.

along the shore, passing from wharf to wharf and housetop to housetop."

Ned stood on the pilothouse of the steamer and waved to his fans. Then he hopped in a boat that took him home to the Island. That night, a gala party was held in Ned's honour. He learned that fans across Canada were donating money to buy him a grand house in mainland Toronto.

Soon after, the Hanlan Club announced that it was no longer needed. Ned's backers had done what they set out to do three years earlier. They kept Ned safe from danger at the hands of gamblers and criminals. They helped him grow from a fisherman's boy to a gentleman and champion. He was now a wealthy, confident sculler who could manage his own affairs. To set Ned on his way, the Club handed over its property to him. It included four racing shells, a boathouse, and the proceeds from the England trip. (The Club members did not deduct their expenses from the earnings of Ned's races.)

Ned's letter to the Hanlan Club was printed in *The Globe*. He thanked the group for their "advice, counsel and wise direction." He wrote, "I cannot forget these loyal friends who, in the long dreary weeks of my training ... stood by me ... and saw me through many difficulties." Ned added that without their help he would not be the champion of Canada, America, and England. He wished the Club could be there for the next part of his career.

Because even though the Hanlan Club was finished, Ned definitely was not.

10 Dirty Tricks

Ned was at a high point in his career, but he was also tired. John Davis, a former member of the Hanlan Club, declared that Ned was in no condition to race. He said: "Hanlan has been in constant training since the Hawdon race in England. He … needs the rest he has so nobly earned."

At home on Toronto Island, Ned relaxed and rowed for fun. A reporter from the *Cleveland Herald* described seeing Ned at this time. An adoring crowd had gathered to watch the champion row. They also hoped for a speech. But Ned joked that his best speeches were made on the water. He pulled away in a racing shell, skimming "over the water just as naturally … as a bird flies through the air."

Not everyone was certain of Ned's fitness. *The Globe* wrote that Ned was "thin and light enough for a hard race, but at the same time … soft and flabby." The article hinted that "the Champion was breaking up."

Though he was not in peak form, Ned raced at the Barrie Regatta on August 18, 1879. He should have stayed home. Some top American scullers raced too. One of them, James Riley, nearly beat Ned. The judges declared the race a dead heat (a draw). The two scullers would have to race again the next day.

Ned was not feeling well. He did not want to take the chance of losing at a small town regatta. He chose not to row in the "race off." The prize money went to Riley.

Ned's near loss was big news. People wondered if his winning streak was over. The American sculler, Charles Courtney, hoped it was.

Ned and Courtney had crossed oars before at Lachine, Quebec, in 1878. During that race, some barges had drifted between the scullers and the finish line. After pausing to get around them, Ned won by just over a boat length. Some American newspapers claimed that Courtney could have easily beaten Ned. The papers also said that the Hanlan Club was dishonest in how it handled Ned's affairs. Ned sent a letter of protest to the editor of *The Mail*. He wrote that the rumours were "without truth … from beginning to end."

In the rematch with Courtney, Ned planned to show Americans that he could beat Courtney fair and square. The eight-kilometre (five-mile) race with a turn was set for October 6, 1879. The course was on Lake Chautauqua in Mayville, New York. The Hop Bitters Manufacturing Company would pay the $6,000 prize. (This kind of sponsorship was new to rowing. Prize money was usually put up by the racers' financial backers, such as the Hanlan Club.)

The scullers arrived in September to train on the lake. A grandstand was built that could seat fifty thousand spectators. An extra railroad line was put along the lake so a train loaded with fans could travel alongside the boats. The hotels were overflowing. People slept on tables and floors. Farmers rented out their haylofts for sleeping quarters. Newspaper reporters followed the scullers around, pens in hand. Some of what they reported was crazy. One wrote that he had learned the secret to Ned's success: a machine hidden inside his boat pushed him along with puffs of air!

The Hanlan-Courtney race promised to be a dazzling event. But when Ned tried to launch his boat, it broke in two. Someone had snuck into the boathouse and damaged it.

The race was postponed until October 16. The night before, Courtney's boathouse guards left their post for a while. When they came back, his racing shells had been sawed in half.

The referee would not postpone the race again. Thousands of people had already put up with one cancelled race. Several fine boats were offered to Courtney, including one of Ned's. Courtney turned them all down. Ned was the only one who showed up at the starting line. He said if Courtney wouldn't race him, he'd row the course anyway to beat the existing record.

The Globe reported: The "gallant little fellow ... [rowed] the fastest time on record, 'just for fun.'

'Good boy, Ned!' shouted Mr. George Williams, of the *New York Herald*.

'Thank you, sir,' replied Ned, cheerily, and spurted for a few strokes just to show what sort of a boy he could be when he tried."

Ned rowed the eight-kilometre (five-mile) course in thirty-three minutes, fifty-six seconds. He set a new record, but was not given the prize money. The sponsor said, "The $6,000 was the prize for a race. Since the race did not take place there could not be a prize."

Courtney's fans went looking for him but he had disappeared. "Courtney is strongly condemned," wrote the *Manitoba Free Press*, "and should he make an appearance, he would be roughly handled."

Later, Courtney accused Ned's people

of sawing the boats. Ned's people (and Ephraim Morris too) said that Courtney's own team had done it so he wouldn't have to race and lose. Why would the guards leave the boats unprotected before such a big race?

Then Courtney accused Ned's friend David Ward, a former member of the Hanlan Club, of offering him money to lose the race. Ned revealed that Courtney's people had offered *him* money to lose. But Ned insisted that no amount of money could entice him to lose, if it were possible to win. On and on it went, with the newspapers calling the Mayville fiasco a "gigantic fraud."

Ned called Courtney a coward. He refused to take back the insult until the American raced him. Finally, Courtney agreed to race Ned in Washington, D.C., in May, 1880. The sponsor agreed to offer the $6,000 prize again on one condition: there had to be an alternate rower. James Riley would join the race if either Ned or Courtney could not row. This way, a race was sure to take place.

The Washington course would be eight kilometres (five miles), with a turn on the Potomac River. It was right behind the White House. Security guards were posted at all times outside the boathouses. People were upset about the Mayville scandal, but about one hundred thousand fans still turned out to watch "The Great Boat Race," as it was called. One of the spectators was the president of the United States!

Ned and Courtney pulled up to the starting line. When Riley saw that the race would take place, he rowed casually up the course towards the turn. *The Globe* reported that as Ned waited for the signal to start, "he looked straight up at the referee, chewing a toothpick ... as though six cents instead of six thousand dollars was all that was at stake on the race." Courtney, on the other hand, "wore a nervous haunted look as though Mr. Blaikie [the referee] had been reading his death-warrant."

The first section of the course curved, so the scullers had a staggered start. When they pulled away, Courtney's boat was far ahead. Ned soon closed the gap and pulled into the lead. Courtney lost his racing stride. He had to stop rowing and restart to get his rhythm back. At the three-kilometre (two-mile) flag, Courtney stopped again and looked to see where Ned was. Ned was far ahead, about to turn his boat around and return to the finish line. His stroke was an easy twenty-seven per minute.

Courtney turned his own boat, and started heading back. Riley saw what he was doing. He pulled into Ned's lane, and took off towards the finish line too. The crowd at the other end was confused. They saw Courtney's boat leading, with Riley suddenly in the race behind him. They didn't know that Courtney had cheated and not raced the full course.

Ned stayed cool. The time had come for him to row flat out. He shot through the water like a bullet and caught up with Courtney and Riley. Then, with the crowd

Ned's homecoming after winning the Championship of England in 1879.

roaring and steamboat whistles blasting, Ned passed them both and crossed the finish line.

The victory should have satisfied everyone. It did not. Riley boasted that he could have beaten Ned fairly if given the chance. That night, some Washington men made Ned an offer. They would raise a prize purse from the public. Two-thirds would go to the winner of the race; one-third would go to the loser. Hanlan agreed.

One week later, Ned raced Riley on the same Potomac River course. Ned rowed without fooling around, and won by almost half a kilometre (one-third of a mile). Finally, the boasts, taunts, and finger-pointing were put to rest. Ned was really and truly the champion of the United States, Canada, and England.

But what about the rest of the world? Far away, in Australia, a tall rower claimed that he was the best anywhere. Ned wanted to prove him wrong.

ROMANCE NOVEL HERO

In the 1800s, there was no television, and newspapers were not yet publishing photographs. Instead, the papers used illustrations and colourful words to bring athletes to life for readers. *The Globe* described Ned in 1880. It said that Ned had a pleasing face, "grand" shoulders, and "a waist like an oak's trunk". The newspaper added: "The muscles of his legs stood out like bunches of cable chains and glided like serpents beneath the bronzed skin that covered them. Such a perfect specimen of manhood ... is seldom seen."

11 Champion of the World

Edward Trickett was a star in Australia, just as Edward Hanlan was a star in Canada. They were alike in many ways. Both used the nickname "Ned." Both had hard-working immigrant fathers. (Trickett's father was an English convict who worked in a stone quarry in Australia.) Both started rowing when they were boys and later became hotelkeepers. Both had once been underdogs in the rowing world. Now both were champions.

Trickett was Australia's first world champion of any sport. He beat the English champion, Joseph Sadler, for the world title in 1876. Back then, Ned was a newcomer wowing the Americans at Philadelphia's Centennial Regatta. After the Sadler challenge, Trickett only raced Australian rowers. He lost some fingers in 1878 when a rolling keg crushed his hand. But Trickett didn't let that slow him down. He continued to beat Australia's best rowers.

Then came the challenge from Ned. Trickett had heard about the Canadian's new rowing style. He also knew about Ned's small size. At almost six foot four, the Australian was a giant compared to "the little Canuck." Trickett agreed to meet Ned on England's River Thames to race for the title of Champion of the World.

As the English watched their two "colonials" train on the Thames, it was the scullers' differences that stood out. Trickett was big and had immense power. The English called him the "colonial Hercules." But Trickett rowed in the old style, using mainly the strength of his upper body to propel the boat. It worked well for short spurts, but was impossible to maintain. Ned's style of rowing, *The London Illustrated Times* wrote, "is simply perfect, and has never been approached by that of any other sculler."

"His sculling," added the *Sporting Life of London,* "was worth traveling a hundred miles to see."

Still, Trickett was confident of winning. Ned said, "When I was training he and his friends were always bluffing and chaffing me."

They boasted, bragged, mocked, and nearly pushed Ned over the edge. But he didn't snap. Losing his temper might mean losing his shot at the championship. He had been banned once before for fouling someone. Now he knew there were better ways to get even. Ned could play some good mind games of his own. But he waited until race day to pay Trickett back.

Many other rowers came to London to see the race. They also planned to row in the International Regatta. It would take place after the Trickett-Hanlan race. Among the scullers were some of Ned's most famous rivals. There was Wallace Ross from Canada, James Riley from the United States, and John Hawdon from England. A large group of Australians brought their support and their money to bet on Trickett. An equally large group of Canadians came to cheer for and bet on Ned. The English were torn. They had seen both men row and knew how good they were. One day Ned would be favoured to win. The next day Trickett would be the number one choice.

Australians bet nearly $100,000 in total

on their man. Canadians matched the wagers. In Toronto, people lined up for two blocks to place bets. Mr. Good (formerly of the Hanlan Club) set up a group wager of $42,000 and wired it to England. Many people had a great deal of money on the line. Ned was offered a bribe of £20,000 to lose the race. But the people of Canada were counting on Ned to win. He would not let them down.

November 15, 1880, was a cold, drizzly day. That did not dampen the spirits of one hundred thousand people who crowded the banks of the Thames. The river was high and rough. Ned, the fisherman, could row in any kind of water. He had two boats with him. One was for smooth water, and one was for rough water. The Queen's own boatman looked after them for him.

Trickett and Ned pulled up to the starting line. "Hanlan," reported the

London Illustrated News, "looked wonderfully well and full of spirits and confidence, while his opponent ... seemed very anxious."

The crowd fell silent as the race umpire called to the men, "Are you ready?" They were. "GO!"

Both men shot ahead. Trickett rowed forty strokes per minute in his short, slashing style. Ned rowed just thirty-six strokes per minute, and soon pulled into the lead. After six minutes, he still looked fresh but Trickett was starting to tire. The crowd's cheers for Ned made him pull even faster. The bow of his shell sped under the bridge "like an arrow on the wing," one reporter wrote. "That structure groaned beneath a dense mass of excited people, who cheered as if each was gifted with lungs of brass."

With each cheer for Ned, Trickett looked more worried. At the five-kilometre (three-mile) mark, the fans were so loud that Ned stopped rowing and waved. Trickett pulled hard to close the gap. Ned picked up his oars again and soon regained the lead. He veered off course. The crowd shouted for him to get back on track. Then Ned spotted William Elliott, the former English champion. He rowed over to chat. The crowd went wild. At one point Ned lay down in his boat and mopped his forehead with a wet sponge. One spectator said that he expected Ned to stand up in his boat and dance the Highland fling.

Each time Ned clowned around,

ALMOST UNBEATABLE

Between 1880 and 1884, Ned won 300 races in a row! In fact, out of about 350 races, he lost only six.

Trickett powered ahead to catch up and pass him. Refreshed, Ned would then speed ahead again.

Suddenly, it seemed as if Trickett might win after all. Ned collapsed in his boat and lay still. Trickett saw this and put every ounce of energy he had left into sprinting toward the finish. The crowd couldn't believe it. Moments before, Ned's win had seemed a sure thing. Now he was about to lose. Thousands of people who had bet on

A regatta at Hanlan's Point on Toronto Island.

him would lose their money.

Just as swiftly as he had collapsed, Ned recovered. He sat up and grabbed his oars. Flashing a smile at the crowd, he easily regained his lead. In the last lengths of the race, he zigzagged casually along, pulling one oar then the other. Whistling steamboats, ringing church bells, and firing canons greeted him at the finish line. The fans who still had voices left cheered for the new World Champion.

THE ART OF THE GAME

Not everyone liked Ned's fooling around. After his race against Trickett, *The London Illustrated Times* wrote: "It is a pity the winner indulged in the clowning business to the extent he did ... Apart from this, Hanlan's exhibition was splendid."

12 The Challengers

It was not long before Ned was challenged for his world title. Right after the championship race, the International Regatta was held in London. Ned was asked not to race in it because he was too good. It would not have been fair to the other scullers. Instead, he put on shows of trick rowing. He could row in a straight line across the river with just one oar.

Australian Elias Laycock won the regatta. Right away he challenged Ned to race for the world title. Laycock was one of his country's best rowers. He had been the Australian champion before Trickett. Ned accepted his challenge. Their conversation was overheard by a reporter. Laycock had one condition: he asked Ned not to embarrass him during the race. Ned agreed.

The race took place on February 14, 1881. As promised, Ned did not embarrass Laycock by stopping to wash his face or visit with friends on the shore. "After all," Ned said, "I didn't want to make a show of a decent plucky man."

Though he took it easy, Ned still won by four boat lengths.

There were no more challengers for a while. They were all too afraid to race Ned. But Ned had other things to keep him busy. He and Maggie had a new baby. Soon he would be teaching her how to swim and row! He also had a new hotel at

Hanlan's Point. He built it the year before with his winnings. Racing took up so much of Ned's time that he had hired a family to run the hotel for him. Now he could spend more time building his business.

People flocked to Hanlan's Point during the summer months. It had the best beach on the Island. Now it also had a superb new hotel. Guests sat on its porches and enjoyed the fresh lake air. Towers on the roof let them take in the beautiful views. There were fun things to do like regattas, children's events, dog swimming races, and concerts. An amusement park was built nearby. It had games, rides, a diving horse, and a fat lady weighing five hundred and ten pounds.

Meanwhile, a rower in England was perfecting his stroke. Robert W. Boyd had been the English champion in 1877. He wanted the title back. He had studied

Ned's winning style, hired Ned's former trainer, and bought a boat like the ones Ned used. The Englishman practiced with the sliding seat. His stroke became long and smooth like Ned's. Some people thought his stroke was even stronger than Ned's. They believed that one day Boyd would beat him.

In early 1882, Ned accepted two challenges. One was from Boyd and the other was from Trickett. Both races would take place in England. The Boyd race was scheduled for April, and the Trickett race for May. Ned arrived in England after Christmas to begin training. He had gained twenty-five pounds, but soon lost it. One of his training tricks was rowing against the tide instead of with it.

Reporters followed Ned like today's paparazzi follow movie stars. They wrote down everything they could about him. Readers gobbled it up. In one instance,

Ned had a "cheerful argument" with the owner of Phelps & Peter's boat builders. A crowd gathered to enjoy the show. Ned wanted the boat builder to make him a shell out of Canadian cedar. The builder insisted there was no such wood. He showed Ned a piece of yellow pine and said, "Do you call that cedar?"

"I guess not," said Ned. "We just cut up that for kindling wood at home."

Another time, a reporter overheard an amateur sculler telling Ned that he should rub rosin into his palms to harden his skin. Ned replied: "'I get hold of my sculls when I am rowing; that knocks the nonsense out of your skin. Look here (showing a palm as tough as a steak cut out of an elephant's hind leg), does that look as if [it] wanted any rosin?'"

On race day, hundreds of thousands of people lined the River Tyne. Boyd had many local supporters who hoped he would win back the Championship of England. And yet very few people placed bets. Deep down, they must have known who would win.

Boyd started well, and even took a slight lead. The crowd cheered him on. Ned soon closed the gap, passed Boyd and left him far behind. Then he slowed down and started clowning around. Fans expected him to do it now. They roared with laughter as Ned made a show of blowing his nose. Boyd rowed as hard as he could to catch up. As soon as he did, Ned spurted

NOT THE AVERAGE BOAT

Paper racing shells were all the rage in the 1870s. They were lightweight but had a short lifespan. Ned preferred cedar boats, but he also tried out new inventions like the fin. It was a small sail attached to the bow. The fin kept boats steady in crosswinds.

away again in the lead. He won the race in twenty-one minutes, six seconds, finishing a few boat lengths ahead of Boyd.

Next, Ned was off to London to race his old rival, Trickett. As the English reporter for *The Globe* put it: "So much for Boyd. Now for Hanlan's next victim."

The rematch with Trickett attracted huge crowds. Once again, hardly anyone

Ned, Champion of the World, on the cover of Canadian Illustrated News.

placed bets. They just came to enjoy the show. Trickett, though, was prepared for a serious race. Trickett had not been in the best shape for his first match with Ned in 1880. He was over-trained and tired. He had hardly slept the night before the race. This time, Trickett was in perfect condition. He thought he had a real shot at earning back the world championship title.

Ned matched Trickett's cocky confidence with his own. He said, "If Trickett rows close after … [me] for a mile and a half, he will have to be 'lifted' out of the boat." He was joking, but in the end, it was not far from the truth.

Trickett still was not good enough to beat Ned. The Canadian crossed the finish line almost a minute and a half ahead of the Australian. Still fresh, Ned sped back to meet Trickett on the course. Then he sprinted again to the finish line, beating Trickett twice in the same race!

For the next two years, other brave scullers challenged Ned for the world championship title. No one could beat him.

A few years later, a ship called *Titanic* would be built. She was the superstar of ships. People thought she was unsinkable. But nothing is perfect. Nothing lasts forever. The *Titanic* hit an iceberg and sank. Ned was like the *Titanic*. He was the superstar of the sporting world. People thought he could not be beaten. They were wrong.

In 1884, Ned and Maggie travelled to Hawaii and Australia. Wherever they went, Ned raced and gave shows of his rowing ability. Crowds flocked to see him. In Australia, everyone wanted to see the little Canadian who had beaten the great Australians, Trickett and Laycock. Ned and Maggie were treated like royalty. They were wined and dined by Australia's high society. A town was named "Toronto" in honour of Ned's birthplace.

Then Ned got sick with typhoid fever, a serious illness that can be fatal. Luckily, Ned was in excellent physical shape. He recovered. As soon as he could, the champion returned to his busy schedule.

On August 16, 1884, on the Parametta River, Ned met his iceberg. Like the other Australians Ned had raced, William Beach was big and strong. He was trained as a blacksmith. People said he had "nerves of steel." Beach challenged Ned to race for the title of World Champion. Confident of winning, Ned accepted.

Beach rowed to win. So did Ned. He tried to get Beach to use up his energy in the first kilometre (half a mile). Beach ignored Ned and rowed at his own pace. Ned's mind games, which worked so well on other scullers, bounced off Beach. Ned had finally met his match. He lost the race. William Beach was now Champion of the World.

13 Coming Home

Within an hour, Ned went from champion to challenger. He marched straight to William Beach's boathouse after the race and asked when they could have a rematch. Beach was in the shower. He called out that he just needed to dry off, then he would be happy to race again!

It seemed that Ned had met his match — in rowing ability and in mind games. The scullers set a date for a rematch. Beach won that race too.

The Australians continued to treat Ned well. Maybe they enjoyed him even more now that an Australian had finally beat him. They gave beautiful gifts to the Hanlans to thank them for travelling so far. Ned said that he had never been treated with such kindness, anywhere in the world.

When Ned and Maggie arrived home in Toronto, there was no parade. Did Canadians feel let down by their "Boy in Blue?" Ned was not ready to give up. He was still an amazing oarsman. He continued to train, race, and win. Crowds kept flocking to see him row. He began racing double-sculls with William O'Connor. They became the American double-sculls champions. But Ned was never able to win back the world champion title for single-scull rowing.

When Ned lost to Beach, something changed in the world of rowing. It lost some of its appeal. Baseball and hockey became more popular with sports fans. The new top scullers did not have the same charm that Ned had. The crowds along the riverbanks and lakeshores got smaller.

In 1890, Ned entered municipal politics. He was the voice of the Islanders and of working people. He also worked at his hotel and spent time with his kids: Edith, May, Grace, Audrey, Margaret, Aileen, Douglas, and Edward Gordon. (The first Edward born to Ned and Maggie died in 1888 as a toddler. Edward Gordon was born in 1890.)

Ned retired from competitive rowing in 1897. He still hung out at the rowing club, gave demonstrations of trick rowing, and told stories about his wild and crazy racing days. H.P. Good, a former Hanlan Club member, said that Ned "never boasted of his skill, but he used to tell the most remarkable stories of his adventures." He recalled Ned telling him about a race in Australia. "After leaving his opponent far behind, he met a man in a boat with a load of hay; stopped the man, climbed on the hay, and after a good snooze, got into his shell again and won by 8 lengths!"

It was said that during the years of Ned's reign, there were five times as many young rowers as there had been before. Ned was in great demand as a coach at schools and universities in Ottawa, Toronto, and New York. His most talented student came from Toronto Island. Eddie Durnan was his sister's son. With the help of his uncle's expert coaching, Eddie became Champion of America, a title he held for many years.

One Christmas, when Ned was fifty-two, he caught a bad cold. It grew worse and became pneumonia. On January 4, 1908, the unstoppable Edward Hanlan died. Toronto and the rest of the country were shocked. Ned had been so full of life. Canadians could not believe he was gone.

Ned was front page news again. The

newspapers were full of stories about his amazing life and career. "Practically he taught the world how to row," stated *The Globe.*

Ned was a living example of the national dream. He had inspired many athletes and working people. They thought of Ned and wondered if their dreams could come true, too. Now he was gone. Ten thousand fans filed past his coffin to say goodbye.

A monument was raised in Toronto to honour Canada's famous sculling son. The bronze statue of Ned towers on its granite

PASSING ON HISTORY

Ned owned a handsome walking stick. It has been passed from one worthy Canadian sculler to the next. Derek Porter was given the cane in 1994. Porter is a former world champion and Olympic medallist. "To have that tie with Ned Hanlan," Porter has said, "was really special."

base. For many years, it stood on the Canadian National Exhibition grounds, watching over Toronto Harbour. In 2004, the monument was moved to Hanlan's Point on Toronto Island. Now it stands near the spot where Canada's first great sports hero rowed as a boy and dreamed of becoming a world champion.

The Ned Hanlan monument at Hanlan's Point on Toronto Island.

Glossary

amateur sculler: a person who rows for fun and pleasure, not for money or work

bootleg: to sell or transport liquor where it is against the law (comes from the practice of smuggling liquor in boot legs)

Canuck: a Canadian

cockpit: the area of a boat where the rower sits

colonial: a person from Canada, Australia, or another country under British rule

double sculls: two rowers on a boat, each with two oars on outriggers

fleet: a group of boats moving together

forfeit: to lose or have to give up because of a penalty

foul: something done against the rules (such as running into another sculler's boat)

gamesmanship: the art of winning using mind games

in-rigged boats: oars rest on the sides of the boat

keel: the main support running the length of the underside of a boat

outrigger: a frame attached to the sides of a boat, which holds the oars

peninsula: a strip of land nearly surrounded by water

Glossary

pitman: someone who works in a mine

prize purse: the amount of money given to the winner of a race

professional rower: a person who rows for work and to earn money

racecourse: the path of a race

racing stride: a rhythmic rowing stroke

rosin: a hard, yellow substance extracted from pine resin that is rubbed on shoes of dancers and boxers to keep them from slipping

scull: refers to both an oar and to the sport of rowing with sculls

shell: a long, narrow racing rowboat

skiff: a small boat

sponsorship: a person or business who provides money for an event

straightaway: a section of racecourse with no turns

swamp: to fill with water and sink

sweep: stretch in a long, wide curve

Toronto Island(s): a cluster of islands in Lake Ontario offshore from mainland Toronto, referred to by locals as simply "Toronto Island" or just "the Island."

Acknowledgements

Telling the story of Ned Hanlan's rowing career is like putting together an old jigsaw puzzle. Some pieces are bent, torn, or missing. Ned loved to tell tall tales, and his fans and reporters made them even taller. It is tricky to sift through the stories and figure out what is true and what is myth. I am grateful to the many people who helped me find and tell Ned's story.

Special thanks to: Albert Fulton from the Toronto Island Archives; the staff at the Toronto Reference Library; the many reporters from *The Globe* and other newspapers quoted in this book; Frank Cosentino for his book *Ned Hanlan* (Fitzhenry & Whiteside, 1978); Sally Gibson, for her book *More Than an Island: A History of the Toronto Island* (Irwin Publishing, 1984); Willow Books for speedily locating copies of the two above out-of-print books; Bill Freeman, for his book *A Magical Place: Toronto Island and Its People* (James Lorimer & Co. Ltd., 1999); Peter Gzowski for his article "Ned Hanlan: the first world champion of anything!" (Great Canadian Sports Stories, Canadian Centennial Library, 1967); David Hurdon for his film *The Toronto Islands Then & Now*; *The Boy in Blue* (a movie with many inaccuracies but which gives a flavour of the time), the following websites:

- www.rowingcanada.org;
- www.rowinghistory.net;
- www.rowinghistory-aus.info;
- www.collections.ic.gc.ca;
- www.argonautrowingclub.com;
- www.toronto.ca;
- www.torontobeach.ca;
- www.archive.comlab.ox.ac.uk (River and Rowing Museum);
- www.hhpl.on.ca/Greatlakes/Documents (Robertson's Landmarks of Toronto);

Anne Powell for helping with the research

and scanning; Rob, Amelia and Maddie Murray and Mom for an unforgettable day on the Island; Hadley Dyer, who asked me to write a Recordbook and guided it to completion, and everyone at James Lorimer & Company Ltd. who helped turn Ned Hanlan's amazing story into *Fire on the Water*.

Thank you all!

Photo Credits

We gratefully acknowledge the following sources for permission to reproduce the images within this book.

• Toronto Public Library, Toronto Reference Library (Canadian Historical Picture Collection): front cover top; back cover top and bottom; 39; 52

• Algonquin Island Archives: back cover middle; 14; 25 (Toronto Marine Museum Collection); 80; 90; 98; 107